Dr. Sana, an orthodontist by qualification has harbored a passion for writing from childhood. Putting pen to paper has been her way of channeling her sentiments.

Her poems reflect her thoughts and observations. Each poem has been written with true intent and honesty. Although profound in content, the simplicity of expression outline some very relevant issues. Poetry must linger in the minds long after being read.

This book creates that impact on the soul.

Dr. Sana Taher

AURORA, THE DAWN

AUSTIN MACAULEY PUBLISHERS™
LONDON · CAMBRIDGE · NEW YORK · SHARJAH

Copyright © Dr. Sana Taher 2022

The right of Dr. Sana Taher to be identified as author of this work has been asserted by the author in accordance with Federal Law No. (7) of UAE, Year 2002, Concerning Copyrights and Neighboring Rights.

All rights reserved. No part of this publication may be reproduced, stored in a retrieval system, or transmitted in any form or by any means, electronic, mechanical, photocopying, recording, or otherwise, without the prior permission of the publishers.

Any person who commits any unauthorized act in relation to this publication may be liable to legal prosecution and civil claims for damages.

The age group that matches the content of the books has been classified according to the age classification system issued by Ministry of Culture and Youth.

ISBN – 9789948809555– (Paperback)
ISBN – 9789948809562 – (E-Book)

Application Number: MC-10-01-0394355
Age Classification: E

Printer Name: iPrint Global Ltd
Printer Address: Witchford, England

First Published 2022
AUSTIN MACAULEY PUBLISHERS FZE
Sharjah Publishing City
P.O. Box [519201]
Sharjah, UAE
www.austinmacauley.ae
+971 655 95 202

To my sister and son.

My sister, for her relentless efforts. Thank you for your belief, unconditional support and love.

My son, who brought in the beacon of hope in my life.

My heartfelt gratitude to my parents.

Thank you for the encouragement and love.

To my brother-in-law, whose kindness and presence made this book plausible.

To my better half, my love, my husband.

Thank you for being a constant inspiration.

And finally, to Almighty, for making this possible and gifting me with this life and words.

Table of Content

Beyond	12
Melancholy	20
Life	31
Essence	44
Woman	49

"The two circumstances where a human unleashes his real self are: one in utter adversity, the other in ultimate power."
                                                      -Sana Taher

Beyond

The Divine

Feeling the sand sink underneath the feet,
Feeling the warm embrace of the setting sun,
Feeling the breeze running through the hair.

Arms open, stretched out wide,
An overwhelming tranquil bliss,
Enclosing in the openness.

The calm waves of the sea,
Gushing gently away,
Rhythm of the heart in sync.

The gulls take flight in the orange blue sky,
The sun sits on the ocean as it appears to slowly go down.

Stars begin to appear and,
The night reclaims its domain.

The waves still gushing,
The breeze still crisp and fresh.

The sea running beyond infinity,
Even in darkness,
Its majestic vastness boggling the mind.

The sea and the sand,
The sky and the stars,
The sun and the moon,
All Divine and immaculate in their presence.

Make us feel minuscule,
Oblivious almost.

Yet we walk on earth like we possess it all,
We want all control,
All the wealth and all the glory.

We have a mind that helps us believe a delusion,
The myth that we have reached the pinnacle.
But, in reality,
We are merely a speck in this vast universe,
We are nothing, but for the divine's creation.

Judge Not

Judge not the color or the race,
Judge not the features of the face,
Judge not the shape or the form,
Judge not the attire or the Grace.
Rather,
Judge for how he treats a child,
Judge the heart and the soul that resides,
Judge the deceptions and the deceit,
Judge the hurt he may besiege.

Judge not the clothes on the back or the shoes on the rack.
Do judge the intent of harm,
And judge the schemes that play.

Judge not a toddler's tantrum,
Judge not a teenager's boredom,
But judge those who judge them.

Judge not the race or the face,
Judge the putrefying ghost that dwells inside.

Black

They say red is the color of love,
I say it is black.
It absorbs all light,
Hides the flaws,
I say it survives.

It is coupled with tragedy and disaster,
I visualize power and individuality.

Red is bright and shines through the night,
Black blends into the darkness.

Stands by when the luminosity fails to shine,
It loves unconditionally,
And conceals the deficiencies away.
Resonates with true love.

It immerses the visible spectrum,
Achromatic without any hue.
Itself obscured; it allows others to shine.
Reminds me of love so virtuous.

They say the color of love is red,
I say it is black.

Human Mind

The human mind, a unique creation, withholds an ocean of thoughts…
From tragedy to triumph, its resilience has dazzled us all…
From the writings of a sonnet to the laws of physics, the human mind deciphers it through…
From vengeance to unconditional love…
A minute creation by God, yet a complex architecture…
Pulp in texture, holds the strength of all seas…
In irony the human mind stands unique…

Inner Child

They say the child in us,
Reminds us to be sane and humane.

The child in us does not divide,
And keeps the hope alive.

The child in us keeps the love afloat,
And hate at bay.

The child in us believes in fairy tales and happy endings.

With curious eyes and a hopeful heart,
The inner child can smile through turmoil.

If only we can keep the child alive,
If only we could see the innocence it reflects in our eyes,
If only each of us could connect to our inner child…

Unsolved Puzzle

Perfection is desired
But never achieved.
Immortality is an illusion
One wants to believe.
Life in itself encompasses
Mystery and distrust.
Human so fragile
Weaker than glass.
The path to redemption
Is a treacherous one.
The walk towards the truth
Is an edgy one.
Maneuvering through this puzzle
Holding diminishing tortures.
Humanity moves to unravel
The dilemma of truth, lies and everything in between.

Melancholy

Trapped

In the deep dark alleys of the mind,
Lie unrelinquished desires.

Hidden in the narrow constrains of the norm,
Survives an anomaly.
Concealed and camouflaged in the ideal,
Dwells a separate need to erupt.

Wearing a cloak of perfection,
Sleeps inside a mismatched soul and mind.

Trapped in this unending battle,
To hide or to reveal.

The internal struggle quenches the heart,
Trapped within the hard shell.
Unable to breathe,
The dreams suffocate within.

Reflecting upon the past helps no more,
Looking at horizon's anew,
May do the trick,
And release the butterflies within.

To breathe in the open skies,
So that these desires remain trapped no more.
What are words?
But, mere concoctions of thoughts.
Setting the words free,
And hence the thoughts are trapped no more.

So Easy

Those smiles so vivid, so vivacious,
That laughter so contagious,
Surrounding the spaces,
The echoes of fun resonating the air.
Yet seem so afar,
So beyond reach.

So easy it is to run over a life and yet smile,
So easy it is to do what you do and,
Yet giggle away.

So easy it is to a snatch a piece,
Of flesh from another and stay content.

So easy for them.
Yet, an improbability for some.
So easy to win by trampling over others.

So easy it is to gain victory through fallacy.

It is a world of shapeshifters,
With very few real souls remaining.
Almost a demonic control over the happenings,
All human and sane logic sleeps buried underneath.

It is the cast of unholy over the saint.
It is almost a demise of good,
And rise of evil.
So easy…

As those who smile through the turmoil,
And pain of others are the one's winning the game.

It is so easy to rip the soul,
So easy to tear one apart to surmount the peak…

Silence

Quiet, deep lull within,
A silence survives inside,
Amidst the nose and chaos,
I find a corner peace inside.
It's deep down,
Way behind.
It stands there,
A close friend, never will it betray,
Never will it go,
Silence stays when all will Leave.
It remains,
Not painful, but beautiful.
Silence makes me love myself,
It knows me and accepts me, for me and only me.
As blissful as it is,
Silence has no loneliness,
It's true and peaceful in its quietness.

Mental Case

She is indifferent, they say,
Then how does she feel too much?
Hear ever decibel?
Sense the truth and spot a lie so soon…?
They say she has walls up,
Then why her mind aches for peace?
Why does she crave love?
Why can she feel the blood drain her heart…?
They say she is a nag,
Then why are her questions not answered?
Why her soul so lonely, and why none can hear her scream…?
He says she is a mental case,
And blames her for her despair,
And entangles her in a web of lies.
She wants to be wanted,
Desires to be needed,
And yet again finds herself begging not to be dismissed.
Just once, aching to be understood.
They say she is indifferent,
Then how are her senses too heightened?
To feel so much…?
They say she has walls up,
But alas, they aren't walls but barriers she can't cross.
He says she is a mental case,
Not knowing the damage he caused…

This story of hurt,
She hides from all,
Keeps it shut from the prying stranger's eyes.
Only to unleash in the darkest of hours,
Screaming at the deaf souls,
To hear her story of solitude.

The Plastics

Perfect lips,
Perfect face,
In a fractured soul.

To attain a structured form,
Plastics are injected.

To achieve a brilliant face,
A surgeon is consulted.
But no cure for a diseased mind,
Or a bleeding heart.

It is a world of people with a perfect exterior,
Covering a distorted interior…

In an Ideal World

Love would be selfless,
Truth would be triumphant,
Kindness would be abundant.

In an ideal world,

Beauty would be timeless,
Health would be desired,
And happiness would be valued.

But alas,
It isn't ideal,
Eyes are deceitful,
Promises are false,
And honesty is despised.

But alas,
It isn't ideal,
Possessions of material are desired,
Liars are throned,
And schemes are planned.

In this facade,
There is a quest for virtue,
An anomaly to be found.

To find the ideal in this lamentable space,
To find forgiveness and tenderness in this ruthless existence.

A true pursuit to attain unadulterated elation.

Life

Think Outside the Box

Confined in narrow spaces of the mind,
Trapped in ideologies so ancient,
All, admire the different.
Yet, reprimand those who practice so.

It is all a herd mentality,
They act and behave alike,
Force children of future to do so.

Yet say,
Think outside the box…

But, why is there a box?
Why are there limitations to imagination?
Why aren't there unending spaces to learn from?
Why can't there be a chance and probabilities of the differential?

Insane are those who think different,
Demented are they who push the boundaries.
Never in their time, but centuries later,
Are they cherished…?
As the normal has no room for unique.

And yet they say,
Think outside the box.
The box they build to contain themselves within.

A Bridge

Life is a long bridge,
High up in the sky,
Connecting the ends of life and death,
Moving with only a breath.
With all the courage I have,
Slow as a snail I move
And dare not look below
For I bear the scare of a fall,
As I finish my first little bit,
I stop and think for what have I achieved,
And when I turn back,
I see all the moments of laughter
And cries happening all over again.
Yesterday is a memory now,
Tomorrow is a day to come.
I wait to know what's in store for me
And every step that I take
I carry nothing with me,
But only bear within my heart
My beautiful memories.

The Contrast

From unending skies to deep blue seas,
From war to peace,
From ecstatic joy to eyes pooled with tears,
From victories at the Rio to the devastate at Aleppo,
From thundering claps to blinding noise of bombs,
From bright lights to pitch dark alleys,
From women fighting for office to women shackled in slavery,
From living to dead,
Every ounce of being surviving with contrast.
The stark differences in corners of the universe.
It is the same world.
The very same humans,
And yet there is a great distinction from ideal to non-ideal…

Tides of Time

Tides of time sweep away,
The moments we lived,
The struggles we survived,
The echoes of laughter and cries.
To engrave in our minds only the memories.
So, from start to finish,
The footsteps we take,
Carve a niche on the sands of time.
For to be remembered,
Or perhaps forgotten.
We walk through space,
Under the starry nights,
To watch our story unfold.
To ponder over the elapsed time,
To forgive and move on.
Neither to wonder over the losses we bore,
Nor to fret over the hurdles we climbed.
But to live,
And walk through the sunset,
To leave footprints on the sands of time.

Hope

Amidst the chaos, there lies hope
At the peak of war, there lies solace, and in ambiguity there lies clarity…
After each night, the sun rises.
There is light, at the end of darkness.
For every end of story, there is a new beginning…
HOPE, to know what's next…
HOPE, to live through this day…
HOPE, to be content at the end.
So, for HOPE we celebrate today…

Destiny

Nothing is lost,
Nothing is gained,
Because life is just a game,
As success seems to shine,
Failure lies just round the line.
If all it is just a play,
Then every life has a story to say.
I want it all,
But I get what I deserve in all.
Someone up there,
Directs us all,
Watching us silently,
He guides us through.
Travelling our paths,
We take our steps.
Filled with hope are we,
Humming the tune of life,
Holding the torch of light,
We find our ways,
To search for the destiny.

My Observation...

The angst in my veins,
Desires the unknown to be drawn.
The madness in my head,
Requires the focus to be sort.
Behind closed doors and silent passages,
There are muffled screams to be heard.
With shifting eyes and mundane gestures,
We walk like zombies…
Our numb-brains being victimized by blinding gadgets,
Social media, we wrap as blankets and pride in self-loathing selfies…
"The world is a smaller place."
Yes, a smaller place with hearts of stone and unresponsive minds…

White Noise

Noise containing many frequencies with equal intensities.
That is the physics of it.
When too many noises audible to the human ear merge at a similar level, it creates white noise.
Much like life itself.
When chaos, noise and opinions are glared at us, it is all blurred into an undeciphered noise,

The White Noise…
The metaphor is uncanny…
And studies show that white noise is calming.

Fake Realities...

Plastered smiles,
Deceptive eyes,
Untrue stories,
Lies weight heavier than facts,
Fake realities we live in.

We say, we like…
But we mean not,
We say we love,
But we hate more…

It is a story,
A web we build,
And then we believe the untrue to be true,
Fake realities we live in…

Trust not even your soul,
The devil resides within,
Believe not even self,
As all is but a facade.
We watch hunger and pain,
We watch death and despair.
Yet do little to none.
None actually care,
Yet pretend to be the saviors.

Fake realities we live in…

Truth is lost in oblivion,
The winners are the best liars,
Honesty ain't the policy anymore.
A rat race of survival it is,
Sadly,
Fake realities we live in…

It Matters

The race doesn't matter,
Winning doesn't matter,
Neither the beginning,
Nor the finish line matters.

Being content matters,
Being at peace matters,
Being happy matters.

We struggle to be the best,
We fight to leave the rest,
And reach the peak,
To achieve tranquility.

But in the rush to ascend,
We fail to imbibe the essence…

For it is the moments that matter,
For it is the seconds of comfort the soul feels in the warmth of love which matters.

For, with an empty heart and a tormented soul,
Mundane, shall be winning.
It is the gratification of being alive that matters.

Essence

The Qasba

The sun glistens upon still waters,
The reflection shimmers as the eyes crinkle.
Amidst the bustling of cars and honks,
The water body embraces the feathered beings.

A place of solace,
Quenching the thirst of dry land.

The carnival around,
The chatter along,
The restaurants surround.

Smell of qahwa,
Engulfs the air.
Enveloping the canal,
Entwined in its soul.
The still waters,
Thrive through joy.
As the sun sparkles diamonds on it.

The Night – All Mine

Times passes by,
Nothing ceases to continue,
Looking through the window,
Imbibing the final ray of the day.
Awaiting the diming of the orange sky,
Stars begin to emerge,
As diamonds on a black stole.
Closure it is of yet another day.
The night's mine,
Solitary I stand,
As I am stripped of the titles,
No mountains to move,
No targets to reach.
The summer breeze,
Flowing through the entangles of my mane,
As I feel elevated through the air.
A sense of calm engulfs around,
Deep breath of a new night I take,
Liberating my soul,
I let my fears free,
To wander in darkness.
City shines through the brilliance of lights,
Sipping my steaming cuppa,
I reflect through the workings of my day.

Full Moon

The moon so white,
Round and bright in its full glory.

Stands majestic,
Brilliant in the dark sky.

Enlightened by the sun, the moon lights up the night.
Although, in its impeccable beauty, it hides a bunny shadow,
Imperfect in its perfection.
It is a night of beauty.

The crisp summer wind,
Flows through,

The glistening, black beauty night,
Has one bright and shining armor.
Standing alone, in its full glory,
Against the contrast sky, it shines on.
For it is a full moon tonight.

Vacant Earth

Empty streets,
Silent walkways,
The quiet serene exterior,
A seething fearful interior.
Maybe it is time we reflect,
It is time we understand,
It is time we figure how miniscule,
How irrelevant we are amidst this colossal universe.
Maybe He is saying don't quarrel over my places of worship,
Instead seek me at your homes, in your hearts,
I reside there.
Beyond borders,
Beyond race and culture,
These times have showed, we are no different.
We are all human.
And that's all we need to be…

Woman

An Enigma

The ocean, as is a heart of a woman,
Deep down under, there in lies the treasure,
So as the secrets enclosed in the eyes of a woman.
Many come by to unravel the mystery,
Yet undiscovered they both remain.
Battleships or coins of gold
Hide deep in the sands below.
The pain of loss or the love for all
Bears a lady in her skin below.
Enchanting and serene, they envelope life within,
If enraged can be a curse unchanged.
As beauty surrounds, they can entice a race along
With their mystique and elegant presence.
The ocean and the lady entangle a man
In the chains of mystery.

Women's Day

An epitome of love and strength, a symbol of life.
Varied roles she plays with ease.
Sails through turmoil and walks through treacherous paths.
Bearing a smile, she waltz through life…
Today we celebrate a creature of beauty and grace, an elegance of existence…
Today we celebrate a WOMAN.

The Lady

Deep within the forest,
There stands a house,
Old and tattered.
Set unique in itself,
There lived a lady,
In it once.
All alone by herself,
No kin did she have,
Her future seemed as dark as the night.
Dawn to dusk she talked to herself,
Loneliness made her a wreck.
And one day when she shut her eyes,
Never to open again,
A young man claimed to be her son.
Alas, he had lost her forever,
Little did he care,
When her heart awaited his company.
Now he stands as they take a mere corpse away,
Just an old pile of flesh, his mother remains.
Busy in his mundane monotony,
His race to make more money,
He lost track of the elapsed time.
Oblivious of the fact that she was growing older.
Now she is gone, never to return,
A vacuum exists,

Unfinished sentences to be spoken.
How he wishes to turn the clock around,
But, silly man, how would he know,
That the hands of time can't be reversed.
A guilt he shall take to grave along…
If only he could do it all over again…

Now She Knows

Solo she walked,
Different she felt,
Can't figure it out,
What singled her out.
Now that she knows,
Her illness is her cure.
A curse or a gift,
She wondered where to shift?
She craved to blend,
Find a common friend.
Yet she stood out,
Different from the lot.
She shall redeem herself,
Her mind will be her grace,
Her heart will find solace.
Now that she knows,
The truth shall be told,
And the story be sold.